How to Use This Book

The **Teaching Versions** of *Elements of Reading: Fluency* will help you guide children to become fluent readers. Because fluency is not an isolated skill but is closely linked to word knowledge and comprehension, each **Teaching Version** contains the following types of teacher support:

- **Fluency teaching suggestions** to help children become proficient in reading with expression (prosody).

- **Word knowledge teaching suggestions** to build children's proficiency in reading words and understanding their structure and meanings. The word knowledge suggestions address recognition of high-frequency words, decoding skills, structural analysis skills, and knowledge of word meanings.

- **Sent ques litera. level.**

- **Story comprehension questions** to help children develop inferential comprehension. Additional comprehension questions are provided in the **Teacher's Lesson Folder**.

After children have completed the repeated reading activities outlined on page 4.4 of the **Teacher's Lesson Folder**, use the reduced **Student Book** pages and teaching suggestions in this **Teaching Version** to provide explicit page-by-page instruction.

Why Cats Hunt at Night

- **Fluency Focus**

    Expression Conveying feelings, mood or characterization

    Punctuation Recognizing that quotation marks signal character speech

    Text Format Understanding that boldface words should often be stressed

- **Word Knowledge Focus**

    Words with long *i*

High-Frequency Words (Boldface words appear in each book of the theme.)

a, again, all, always, and, around, as, at, away, big, but, can, could, **day**, good, got, grew, her, how, in, it, made, never, **night**, not, once, one, said, **see**, she, **sleep**, so, soon, the, then, there, **they**, time, to, too, up, upon, very, was, we, went, what, when, why, with, you

- **Sentence Comprehension Focus**

    Comprehending stated details

- **Story Comprehension Focus**

    Identifying cause and effect

Why Cats Hunt at Night

Written by Claire Llewellyn
Illustrated by Simona Dimitri

Harcourt
Supplemental Publishers
Rigby · Steck-Vaughn
www.steck-vaughn.com

Getting Started

To begin, read the title page aloud or invite a volunteer to do so.

Book Summary

In this *pourquoi* tale explaining the nocturnal nature of cats, Cat is not a good hunter because she hunts in the day, when her prey can see her. One bright moonlit night, however, she washes her face in a silvery pond and gets big, shiny eyes. After that, she can see at night and is a good hunter.

■ Fluency

Point out the familiar introductory phrase "Once upon a time." Then direct children's attention to the comma after the phrase. Explain that the comma signals that the reader should pause slightly before going on with the rest of the sentence.

Point out the two commas in the third sentence. Invite a volunteer to read the sentence correctly, pausing between the names of the animals.

■ Word Knowledge

Direct children's attention to the word "time." Point out the *i*-consonant-*e* pattern in the word, which signals the long *i* sound. Ask children to find the other word that has the same pattern ("mice").

Once upon a time, there was a cat.
Cat hunted in the day.
She hunted mice, birds, and frogs.

■ Sentence Comprehension

Ask   *What does Cat do in the day?* (hunt)

2

At night, Cat went to sleep.

3

■ Sentence Comprehension

Ask *What does Cat do at night?* (go to sleep)

■ Fluency

Point out the comma in the sentence after the introductory phrase "At night." Invite a volunteer to read the sentence correctly, pausing slightly at the comma before going on with the rest of the sentence.

■ Word Knowledge

Focus children's attention on the theme high-frequency words *day*, *night*, and *sleep* on pages 2–3. Invite a volunteer to write the words on the board. Tell children that they will see these words in all three of the books about day and night.

Have a volunteer add *see* to the list on the board. Have children read the word aloud and find it on the page. Tell children they will see the word in all the books in this theme.

Cat was not good at hunting.
The mice, birds, and frogs could see her.
"We can see you, Cat!" said the mice.

■ **Sentence Comprehension**

Ask   *Why is Cat not good at hunting?* (The mice, frogs, and birds can see her.)

4

"We can see you!" said the birds.
"Cat, we can see you!" said the frogs.
And they always got away.

5

■ Sentence Comprehension

Ask *What do the mice, birds, and frogs tell Cat?*
("We can see you!")

■ Fluency

Point out the quotation marks in the sentences on pages 4–5. Review with children what quotation marks tell a reader—that a character or characters are speaking.

Guide children to recognize that the speakers are taunting Cat. Then ask children how they should read the words in quotation marks to let a listener know that the animals are teasing Cat. Point out the exclamation marks if necessary. Then have children read pages 4–5.

■ Word Knowledge

Focus children's attention on the high-frequency word *they*. Point out the word as one that appears in all three books about day and night. Have a volunteer add it to the list on the board. Ask children whom *they* refers to (the mice, birds, and frogs). Have children read the list aloud.

■ Fluency

Ask the children to read the page silently and decide how to use their voice to convey that Cat's life is not going well. Have volunteers share their interpretation.

■ Word Knowledge

Focus children's attention on the word "tired." Ask children to tell what the word means ("wanting rest or sleep; lacking energy"). Explore with children ways in which they know someone is tired.

Cat was always hungry.
Soon she was very, very tired.
One day, she was too tired to hunt.

6

■ Sentence Comprehension

Ask *Why does Cat not go hunting?* (She is too tired.)

Cat went to sleep and slept all day.
When she woke up, it was night.

7

Have students recall what happens next in the story. Suggest that they try to read the second sentence in a way that hints at the mysterious silver pond with water that changes Cat's eyes.

■ Word Knowledge

Refer children to the list of theme high-frequency words on the board. Ask children to study pages 6–7 and to find the words *sleep*, *day*, and *night*.

■ Sentence Comprehension

Ask *When does Cat wake up?* (at night)

■ **Fluency**

Point out the exclamation marks after the sentences. Remind children that exclamation marks indicate sentences to be read with great feeling.

■ **Word Knowledge**

Point to the word *night* in the list of theme high-frequency words on the board. Ask children to find the word *night* on the page.

How dark the night was!
How big and shiny the moon was!
How silver the moon made the pond!

■ **Sentence Comprehension**

Ask *Why does the pond look silver?* (The moon shining on it makes it look that way.)

Cat went to the silver pond.

She washed her face.

Then she washed her eyes.

9

Remind children of the importance of this part of the story: in this part, Cat gets big, shiny eyes. Talk with children about how they can use their voice to convey the mystery in this part of the story. Allow children to share their oral interpretation of pages 8–9.

■ **Sentence Comprehension**

Ask *What does Cat wash?* (her face and eyes)

Cat's eyes grew big and shiny.
They grew as big and shiny as the moon!

10

■ Fluency

Ask children what clue at the end of the second sentence tells how it should be read. Invite a volunteer to read the sentence.

■ Sentence Comprehension

Ask *What happens to Cat's eyes?* (They become big and shiny.)

Cat looked around with her big, shiny eyes.
She could see in the dark!

11

Talk with children about how Cat probably feels at this point in the story (excited). Have them experiment with using their voice to convey how Cat feels.

■ **Word Knowledge**

Have children read the list of theme high-frequency words on the board aloud. Ask children to find the word that appears on the page.

■ **Sentence Comprehension**

Ask   *What happens when Cat looks around?*
         (She discovers she can see in the dark.)

Point out the question mark at the end of the first sentence. Ask children what their voice should do at the end of that sentence (go up). Invite a volunteer to read the question in a way that shows how *not* to read it. Then have the volunteer read it correctly.

And what could Cat see with her shiny eyes? She could see the mice.

12

She could see the birds.
She could see the frogs.
But they could not see her!

13

■ Sentence Comprehension

Ask   *What can the mice, birds, and frogs not do?*
(see Cat)

■ Fluency

Call children's attention to the two words on the page that are darker than the other words. Explain that this dark type tells a reader that those words are to be read with more force. Invite children to explain why those words should be read in that way (to point out that what the animals can do is the opposite of what Cat can do).

Point out that the exclamation mark in the last sentence signals that it should be read with excitement. Invite a volunteer to read the sentence aloud.

■ Word Knowledge

Ask children to find the theme high-frequency words on pages 12–13.

Cat hunted all night.
She hunted mice, birds, and frogs.

■ Fluency

Ask children how Cat probably feels at this point in the story (happy she can find food). Have them use their voice to convey Cat's happiness. Invite volunteers to share their oral interpretation.

■ Sentence Comprehension

Ask *What does Cat do all night?* (hunt)

Soon it was day .

Cat was tired, so she went to sleep .

15

Direct children's attention to the list of high frequency words on the board. Ask children to find the ones that appear on pages 14–15.

■ Sentence Comprehension

Ask *When does Cat go to sleep?* (in the day)

Invite volunteers to read the page aloud to show the story's happy ending (for Cat, at least). Make sure they pause after periods. Encourage children to read the last sentence in different ways. Ask them to decide on the best way to read the sentence to let a listener know that the sentence is the end of the story.

Cat was very good at hunting in the dark. She was never hungry again.

And that's why cats hunt at night and sleep in the day.

16

■ **Sentence Comprehension**

Ask   *Why isn't Cat ever hungry again?* (She is very good at hunting in the dark.)

■ Story Comprehension

Ask *At the beginning of the story, why isn't Cat good at hunting?*
(The mice, birds, and frogs can see her.)

Ask *What happens because Cat is not a good hunter?*
(She becomes hungry and tired.)

Ask *What happens after Cat washes her face?* (Her eyes become big and shiny.)

Ask *At the end of the story, why is it good for Cat that the other animals cannot see her?* (She can hunt them and eat them.)

Ask *How does Cat change in the story?* (She becomes good at hunting.)

■ Fluency Flip Page

The **Fluency Flip Page** of the **Student Book** contains a passage from the book to facilitate timed reading. For more information on timed reading and other ways of assessing fluency, see the **Teacher's Lesson Folder.**

Once upon a time, there was a cat. — 8

Cat hunted in the day. — 13

She hunted mice, birds, and frogs. — 19

At night, Cat went to sleep. — 25

Cat was not good at hunting. — 31

The mice, birds, and frogs could see her. — 39

"We can see you, Cat!" said the mice. — 47

"We can see you!" said the birds. — 54

"Cat, we can see you!" said the frogs. — 62

And they always got away. — 67

Cat was always hungry. — 71

Soon she was very, very tired. — 77

One day, she was too tired to hunt. — 85

Cat went to sleep and slept all day. — 93

When she woke up, it was night. — 100